God, a Rich Supply of All Good
by Nathaniel Holmes
with chapters by C. Matthew McMahon

Copyright Information

God, a Rich Supply of All Good, by Nathaniel Holmes, with chapters by C. Matthew McMahon
Edited by Therese B. McMahon and Susan Ruth

Copyright © 2021 by Puritan Publications and A Puritan's Mind

Some language has been updated from the original manuscript. Any change in wording or punctuation has not changed the intent or meaning of the original author(s), and has been made to aid the modern reader.

Published by Puritan Publications
A Ministry of A Puritan's Mind®
Crossville TN
www.apuritansmind.com
www.puritanpublications.com

All rights reserved. No part of this publication may be reproduced, stored in a retrieval system or transmitted in any form by any means, electronic, mechanical, photocopy, recording or otherwise, without the prior permission of the publisher, except as provided by USA copyright law.

This Print Edition, 2021
Electronic Edition, 2021
Manufactured in the United States of America

ISBN: 978-1-62663-401-5
eISBN: 978-1-62663-400-8

Table of Contents

God is Good..4

Meet Nathaniel Holmes.....................................11

Part 1: God, a Rich Supply of All Good.........14

Part 2: God's Gracious Thoughts Towards Great Sinners..36

Part 3: God's Gracious Expressions............59

Other Helpful Works Published by Puritan Publications..81

God is Good
by C. Matthew McMahon, Ph.D., Th.D.

"And, behold, one came and said unto him, Good Master, what good thing shall I do, that I may have eternal life? And he said unto him, Why callest thou me good? there is none good but one, that is, God," (Matt. 19:16-17).

As with the Rich Young Ruler, people base what they see others do, *i.e.* external acts of their own observing and evaluating, as what they deem to be *good*. When the young man came to Jesus, he first *compliments* him about Jesus' good works, and then proceeds to ask him about how he might gain eternal life (in fact *inherit* it, *cf.* Mark 10:17ff and Luke 18:19ff). He had heard and seen Jesus do many *good* things, from *his* point of view. Jesus then takes time to teach this young man about the law of God and the commandments of God which, truly, teach a man what is good and what is not.

What does it mean to *be good?* Dictionary definitions are always helpful; Webster defines "good" as anything, "virtuous, righteous and commendable." We may have what we consider to be good food, good friends, a good car, a good house, *etc.*, things that we believe have certain admirable qualities. But this is not the same as *the goodness of God*.

The goodness of God is that where in his self-manifestation, he is thought of in two ways: 1) absolutely and in himself as supremely good and perfect, and the only good because he is good originally, perfectly, and immutably that way. But, also, because he is: 2) outwardly good as beneficent towards his creatures (something the rich young ruler saw as a *more* important trait). But Jesus points out, in harnessing the law of God, that God is good inwardly first, and then outwardly second.

In the first way, God is good in being. That simply means, what is right according to his character. God is benevolent generally in his indiscriminate providence over the whole earth. "The LORD is good to all: and his tender mercies are over all his works," (Psa. 145:9). The sun still shines each day and the moon still revolves around the earth – those are *good* acts. This means God does not act with evil or malice. Inwardly he always acts according to his nature, and outwardly this is seen by the beneficent acts he does for the good of creation. In fact, when he created everything, he saw all that he did and created as "very good," (Gen. 1:31).

In the second way that God is good, it extends to his creatures in three different ways, preservation, providence and election. First, he preserves both man and beast in their stations of life. Cows, bugs, birds, men, children, whales, *etc.*, are all upheld and exist by his power. Everything, "indeed was very good," when he created all things according to their kinds and stations.

Even after the fall, cows do not become bad (though they are part of fallen creation), and they are still upheld in their nature as a created entity. God continues to sustain them. Even wicked men are upheld in their beings. God does not instantaneously destroy humankind because of the fall. In his indiscriminate providence he makes apples grow on trees and people eat those apples; the rain falls and the sun shines (Matt. 5:45). God, in making apples, is good, because making apples is not evil.

Lastly, God communicates his goodness to his elect. Abraham was called a friend of God (James 2:23). God communicated his *goodness* to Abraham, so Abraham could receive the greatest amount of happiness he was capable of receiving at the time. The goodness of God produces all the happiness to be gained in the entire universe, and this is the view of Genesis 1–2, when it records that God, "saw it was good." In the manner in which a good God relates to those who are not elect, they are given *good things*, but the intention behind those things is of another design. God gave Esau a father (and that was a good thing), a home (and that was a good thing), a mother (and that was a good thing), a brother (and that was a good thing), family, talents, livestock, as a matter of fact, whatever Esau had, God had given him. But Esau was not one of God's elect. The ultimate disparity of the event of Esau's non-election, then, demonstrates the *intention of God* in giving Esau good things. Their intention is a far different thing for him than Jacob's good things as one of God's beloved.

For Esau, those good things were a further aggravation of his decent into the fury of hell. Good things had a bad outcome for him.

The goodness of God serves two functions among the divine perfections of God. First, it demonstrates his being; second, it is the primary affection of God's divine will. Make this notation – *all happiness comes from God*. Such happiness is to manifest his glory. It is to demonstrate the highest moral excellence that his creatures should desire. It is to give his elect (and the renewed creation) the highest attainment of blessedness in Christ Jesus that they could receive.

Everyone wants God to be good to them. Who would ever say otherwise? The goodness of God is something most *secularized churches* harp upon, and this is actually not to their shame (Mark 9:39). It's wonderful that people look to the goodness of God and praise God for it. However, it's not so good if they don't know what it *means* that, "God *is* good." Generally, the secularized church gets their theology from songs by people like Velna Ledin who wrote a song called, "God is so Good," in 1933, about the time that pithy praise songs started to gain momentum. Here are the complete lyrics to the song:

> God is so good,
> God is so good,
> God is so good,

God is Good

He's so good to me!

The "song" is based on 1 Chronicles 16:34, "O give thanks unto the Lord, for He is good," and was composed to "pass the time on a road trip." Is this akin to *99 bottles of beer on the wall?* That was used to pass time as well. What does this song actually mean?

Or what do you think about the child's prayer we hear so very often?

God is Great, God is Good;
Let us thank Him for our food.
By His hands we all are fed,
Give us Lord our Daily Bread.

Without having a context and a teaching, these mean little to nothing to people, though they *are* true on a basic level. Yet, not only do they mean little, but they are reversed in their theological explanations. From the way the song is written, or the prayer is prayed, God is so good *because* he is *so good to me*, or *gives me food.* But this is opposite to what Jesus taught in Matthew 19. He asked the question, "Why do you call me good?" This was to put the pointed end on these questions as to what the song means and what the prayer means. The song and child's prayer makes goodness an outward observable act *to me*, or *for me*. However, Jesus corrects this thinking, showing that God is good because he is full of his own goodness, not simply because he is good to me. If we minimize the song or prayer, they simply say, "God is so good to me." But that is not *why* God is good. If nothing existed other than God, as it was before creation, God was still good, has always been good, will be good forever, and does not need anything in creation to be or act as good because he is intrinsically good in and of himself eternally. God alone is good, and good to all, but not to all alike.

Nathaniel Holmes will take this very sound and important theological idea of God being *good*, and apply it readily to the people of God. At the outset, he says, "The fountain of all rich supplies is God who is infinite and can supply all needs infinitely. The conveyance and insurance are infallible, as they are found in Christ Jesus." All the supplies that come from God through Christ to those of God's elect who are *in Christ*, come enriched with God's glory shining all over them. Holmes explains that providences below, graces within, heaven above all have a lovely scarlet blush of Christ's blood upon them, so that rays of divine love shine on those who are in Christ. What a most excellent topic for the Christian to be encouraged and revived by!

After Holmes lays out that God is in fact good, and a glorious supply of goodness in Jesus Christ, he then deals with Isaiah 55:8-9, "For my thoughts are not your thoughts, neither are your ways my ways, says the Lord. For as the heavens are higher than the earth, so are my ways higher than your ways, and my thoughts than your thoughts." He shows that this chapter is a most glorious invitation to poor sinners to obtain free mercy. In this he teaches that the incomparable nature of God's gracious thoughts toward poor sinners, is above and beyond their own thoughts, and is sufficient to stop the mouth of all objections and still the cries of all sadness and all miseries.

In the third and last section, Holmes shows God's gracious expressions engaging himself with those that accept his grace.[1] He takes this from 2 Cor. 1:3-4, "Blessed be God, even the Father of our Lord Jesus Christ, the Father of mercies, and the God of all comfort; who comforts us in all our tribulation, that we may be able to comfort them which are in any trouble, by the comfort wherewith we ourselves are comforted of God."

In this delightful study of God's holy word, may you be refreshed and encouraged to hold steadfastly to the goodness of God in Christ in all things that he bestows on his people, as the Father of mercies, the God of all comfort, for his glory and the good of his people.

In Christ's glorious goodness and grace,
C. Matthew McMahon, Ph.D., Th.D.
From my study, January, 2021
John 5:39, "...search the Scriptures..."

---

[1] Keep in mind that the word "accept" to the puritans was far different than to evangelical Christianity today. Accept, for the reformers and puritans, was akin to *receive*.

Meet Nathaniel Holmes
Edited by C. Matthew McMahon, Ph.D., Th.D.

Nathaniel Holmes (or Homes) (1599–1678) was an English puritan, covenanter and prolific Calvinistic writer. He is described as, "a Puritan writer of great ability," and a scholar. He is praised to have been well skilled in Hebrew.[2]

He was son of the Rev. George Holmes of Kingswood in Gloucestershire. He was born in 1599 in Wiltshire. After his conversion to the Gospel of Jesus Christ, he went to college to study on April 11, 1617 as a fellow-commoner of Magdalen Hall, Oxford, where he later moved to Exeter College. He was admitted to the school in order to earn a B.A. (which he did on October 19, 1620). It seems that he then returned to Magdalen Hall, in order to earn another degree, a Master of Arts, in 1623.[3] He had previously become a frequent preacher in the neighborhood of Oxford, desiring to serve the Lord Jesus Christ on bended knee as a preacher of the word. Later, he earned degrees in divinity, a B.D. in 1633, and a D.D. in 1637, as a member of Exeter College. He was strongly Calvinistic, and among the earliest of the ministers who subscribed to the *Solemn League and Covenant*.

---

[2] Kennett's *Eccles. Chron.* i. 553, 827; Palmer's *Nonconf. Mem.* i. 149; Wood's *Athenæ Oxon.* ed. Bliss, iii. 1168; Atkyns's *Gloucestershire*, ed. 1768, p. 259; Boase's *Register of Exeter College*, p. 250.
[3] Oxford University *Reg.*, Oxf. Hist. Soc., II. ii. 360, iii. 388.

In 1643 he was presented to the rectory of St. Mary Staining. Holmes soon changed his views, and, becoming a millenarian, joined Henry Burton, B.D., minister of St. Matthew's, Friday Street, in establishing an independent congregation towards the end of 1643. Mr. Wood states that he had several congregations in the country, which he visited from time to time: one of them was at Dover.[4] Mr. Pepys seems to have gone to hear Holmes preach at Whitehall on February 12, 1659.[5] On the enforcement of the *Act of Conformity* in 1662, Holmes gave up his position with those churches, and went to reside in the parish of St. Giles, Cripplegate, where he either kept or frequented conventicles. He died in June of 1678, and was buried in St. Mary, Aldermanbury.

The *works* of Nathaniel Holmes, D.D. are the following, three of which have been updated by Puritan Publications* (which include this current work):

1. "Usury is Injury," London, 1640, 4to.
2. "Vindication of Baptizing Believers' Infants, in some Animadversions upon Mr. Tombes, his Exercitations about Infant Baptisme," *etc.*, London, 1646, 4to.
3. "Dæmonologie and Theologie,* the first the Malady, etc., the second the Remedy," *etc.*, London, 1650, 8vo.

---

[4] *Athenæ Oxon.* ed. Bliss, iii. Page 1168.
[5] See his *Diary* i. page 27.

4. "The Mischiefe of Mixt Communions fully discussed," etc., London, 1650, 4to.

5. "Song of Solomon. A Commentary on the whole Book of Canticles," 1650, 8vo.

6. "Ecclesiastica Methermeneutica, or Church Cases cleared," 1652, 8vo.

7. "The Resurrection revealed, etc.: I. That Chiliasme, or the opinion of the future glorious state of the Church on earth is no errour. II. Of the manner and measure of burning the world. III. Touching Gog and Magog. IV. Concerning Covenants," *etc.*, London, 1661, fol.

8. "Exercitations on the Chiliasme, the Burning of the World, of Gog and Magog, the two Witnesses, and the Character of Antichrist," London, 1664, fol.

9. "Miscellania; consisting of three treatises: I. Exercitations extricated, etc. II. A Review of, or a fresh Enquiry after Gog and Magog, where to find them. III. Some Glimpses of Israel's Call approaching," etc., London, 1666, fol. 10. "An Essay concerning the Sabbath," London, 1673, 8vo.

10. "God, A Rich Supply of All Good,"* 1650.[6]

11. "God's Gracious Thoughts Towards Great Sinners,"* (1647).

---

[6] *God, A Rich Supply of All Good*, by Nathanael Homes (1599-1678), Setting forth: 1. The believer's interest in it. 2. The riches of it in quantity. 3. The gloriousness of it in quality. 4. The means of sealing it all up: namely, Christ. All illustrated, with many wonderful and remarkable spiritual experiences, not only of former, but of later Christians. (London: Thomas Roycroft, 1650).

Part 1:
God, a Rich Supply of All Good

Phil. 4:19, "But my God shall supply all your need, according to his riches in glory, by Christ Jesus."

This is a rich and glorious text, for it contains riches and glory. It is a comprehensive text, for it speaks of supplying all need. The fountain of all these rich supplies is God who is infinite and can supply all needs infinitely. The conveyance and insurance are infallible, as they are found in Christ Jesus. And the impression that all these make upon the heart of a believer is significant. In addition, the text is spoken out of much confidence and experience: "*my* God shall supply. *My God that has supplied me,*" (verses 12, 13). For this reason, Paul assures that this same God *shall* supply you. The word "but" in verse 19 in our English translation may be better translated "thus." That is, "God has heretofore supplied me," (verse 13). Now "you have supplied me," (verse 14, 16). And *thus,* "God shall supply you."

Question: Why did Paul not refuse the Philippians' benevolence, and turn "your" into "my," and his words to others into faith for himself, saying, "my God shall supply all *my* need."

Answer: Paul could, and had, and would again have done this, if God had denied all means. But for him to refuse means when means were offered would be to tempt God and not trust in him. The Philippians had plenty to spare, and (contrary to the greedy Corinthians) were willing to share.

Paul fulfilled his ministry, sharing richly those doctrines of God and the gospel with the Philippians. Therefore, the Philippians did well to give, and he did well to receive, what he needed in return. Besides, Paul had received from them a small contribution of some temporal things; but he promises them that his God should supply all the needs of them all, both spiritually and temporally. "My God shall supply all your need, according to his riches by Christ Jesus."

Shall supply, in the Greek, means "shall fill," or "will fill." He shall, because he will. His good will puts a necessity on his great power to do great things for his people – the fundamentals of salvation, of grace and glory that God does for his own in and by Christ Jesus (Eph. 1:1-10). And why? Because he had taken counsel with his will so to do (verse 13) in all providences and in all things, (Rom. 8:28-29). Make a note here the joining word "for" that knits these two verses together. And as his will is a good will, it is also a rich good will. "According to his riches," (the text says.) He is rich for our need; and has riches for *every* need. And richly shall he proportion the allowance, namely, "according to his riches in glory."

The joining glory to riches signifies that God will supply according to his riches *gloriously;* or rather it signifies *more*, so that he will supply according to his *glorious* riches. All the supplies that come from God through Christ to those of us who are in Christ, come enriched with glory. Providences below, graces within, heaven above. They all have a lovely scarlet blush of Christ's blood upon them, so that rays of divine love shine on those who are in Christ.

And whether we render the text *in Christ*, or *by Christ*, or *with Christ*, it makes no great difference. For according to Scripture *all* are true, and *all* will concur to clear the way for us to receive all things that are ours through Christ. Regarding Christ's passion, we have access to all things by Christ, namely, by the purchase of his blood (Eph. 1:11-12). Regarding Christ's incarnation, we have access to all things in Christ because of our union with him (1 Cor. 1:5, John 15:5, Col. 2:10). Regarding that union, we have access to *all things* with Christ. That is, God gives us to Christ in spiritual marriage. In so doing, with him he gives us *all* his estate with him (Rom. 8:32).

For these reasons, the doctrine may be stated in this way, that believers have assurance and experience that their God will fully supply all their need according to his glorious riches through Christ Jesus.

There are four things requiring explanation in the order in which they lie in this doctrine for both the manifestation and the confirmation. 1.) The believer's interest in the supplier that makes him so bold and confident as to say, "my God shall do so and so." 2.) The extension in quantity of the supply: to supply all need. 3.) The intension in quality, according to his glorious riches. 4.) The medium or means, which is Christ Jesus.

1. The interest. The believer *has* God, the only true God, who is the origin of all things. All manner of goodness is nothing but copies of that original. All streams of

goodness are from that ocean of nectar. "All my springs are in thee," says the psalmist in Psalm 87:7. That is, all my resources and refreshment and nourishment are from God. All things are in God, whether formally or causally or eminently. Wisdom, power, *etc.*, are so formally in God, that they are essentially God. All the creatures are causally in God; that is, they have their being from an efficacy proceeding *from* him. And all the rest are eminently in God. Whatever is excellent below is in God in a more excellent manner, as light is more excellent in the sun than in a fire or candle. God is the divine artist to know all. He is the divine artificer to make all (Hebrews 11). And, he is the divine virtuous one, to do all. As it is said of Christ, he did *all things well.* We act well, being well acted of him. His omnipotent power upholds all. His all-loving heart gives all. And his all-wise hand dispenses all. His power is above all difficulties. And his good will above all our unworthiness.

You see the world below is virtually in the sun; and the sun is a more excellent thing than all on which it has an influence. So, all things are much more eminently in God, but God himself is more excellent than them all (Psa. 84:11). His nature is inaccessible. He dwells in light that none can approach. His love is incomprehensible (Eph. 3). And his ways of works and providences are past finding out (Rom. 11). He supplies the angels that did not fall with power that they might *never* fall. He supplied Christ, filling him with the Spirit above measure and raising him from the dead. Therefore, he is able to supply his own with everything *and more* that they need.

In this God the believer has his interest. He can confidently call him, "my God," mine by creation. And not only of being, but of his wellbeing, of a gracious heart, and gracious qualities in that heart (Psa. 51:10, Eph. 4:24, Eph. 2:10). He is, "my God," by preservation, and not only in common providences, as he is the Savior of all men; but in preservation of my soul from sin, of my affections from prevailing temptations, and graces to spare me eternal death. He is, "my God," by redemption. Christ is made of God to us redemption (1 Cor. 1). He paid a price to redeem us from the wrath of God for sin and has gained the actual love of his mercy to bestow all good upon us.

Upon these grounds, and in this manner the believer challenges God to be *his God.* The believer says, "God is my God," fundamentally by the promise. And God affirms, "I will be your God, and you shall be my people." Formally and properly by faith, "my beloved is mine, and I am his," (Song of Songs 2). As Thomas says, "my Lord and my God." Effectually, by the operations of love, joy, etc., as Mary said, "my spirit has rejoiced in God my Savior." This the believing Jews did in 1 Peter 1:8. When we own God, and own ourselves to be no others but his, faith draws Christ down to us. And that faith working by love, carries us up to Christ. Song of Songs 2 says, "my beloved is mine, and I am his, he feeds among the lilies until the daybreak, and the shadows flee away…"

2. Extension in quantity. God shall supply, even to a fulfilling of all needs. The word here rendered *need:*

1. Signifies lack or necessity. So that whatever is necessary to supply, God will supply. A sinless lacking, namely, of those things without which we cannot answer to God's ends, God will be sure to supply. But a sinful lacking, an immoral thirst for those things that will rather hurt than help, God does best to keep us lacking than supplying. It is better for us that he withholds rather than supplies. Psalm 119 says, "It is good for me that I was afflicted." In this case we need soul health more than bodily supplies; therefore, God withholds creature-comforts that he might cure our spiritual shortages. Many of our natural desires are either after things that are not good for us, or in degrees unsuitable for our condition. In addition, our needs must be real, not imaginary as was the dream of thirst in the prophet. Such an imaginary want was also in Rachel when she fantasized that her life depended upon having children. "Give me children," she said, "or I die."

2. The Greek word *need* signifies *use, i.e.,* that which is useful and instrumental to act and do. In other words, what is needful for our true use and that fits us for God's use. For we are God's instruments, his reasonable tools. As noted in Revelation 4, all is made for God's end and use; therefore, without fail, God will so supply and serve our need as may suit us best to serve him.

And in relation to both meanings of the word, remember that I told you that the word *supply* in the original signifies, "to fill." God will at least fill the true useful need. He may and does often make our cup to overflow, giving a measure running over of superabundant kindness.

But this he will do, because he is tied by his covenant and seal, in word and sacraments to fill such wants. He will fill every size vessel, replenish every capacity to its proportion. He will ballast and tackle every ship, that it may safely ride out every storm. He clothes his lambs and sheep with a fleece they may best wear to be spared injury from the thorns.

3. Intention in qualities, one way or other, first or last, he will supply according to his glorious riches. God is glorious, and so will dole out your share according to your proportion. In comparison, you shall have great things. As James says, "God has chosen the poor of this world to be rich in faith." And Paul says, "godliness is great gain with contentment." God brings contentment, ease of heart, and more satisfaction than the entire world can offer. The godly man has access to two worlds. Godliness has the promise of this world *and* that to come. Knowing this, the godly man can say, "I have enough." He is rich that lacks nothing more than bread sufficient for sustenance. A man's estate is to be valued according to the *use*, not the *bulk*, according to the *efficacy* not the *quantity*. Of what value are tools that one has no use for or is not benefitted by? If a man's estate serves his need and is good for his spirit, he has everything that can be desired.

The whole of a believer's estate is very rich, *because:*

1. The least mercy is greater than all creature comforts, for a man is all misery left to himself.

2. No matter how little it is, Christ is of more value than all the rest combined.

3. Even if the stream of mercies is small, great is their continuance from the fountain.

4. Besides, the believer has the fountain itself, God himself. The godly man has not only the light, but the sun itself fixed in him as in its orb. The Christian and God are one, as Christ and God are one (John 14:20, John 17:21). All that God gives to believers is intended in the end to lead them closer to God. God is a wooer of men who gives tokens of his love to show his intent to give himself.

You see how God does richly supply in many ways. And that richness that God supplies is a glorious richness. This glory is three-fold, as the riches are three-fold.

1. There is a glory in the supply of the temporal needs of the believer in that they come from God's right hand and from his good will, not from mere common providence. They all taste lavish; they are varnished with love; they are polished with the beauty given to Christ for us. This glory in the seasonable supplying of the believer's temporal needs is like *apples of gold with pitchers of silver*. Striped with the blood of Christ, inlaid with the operation of the Spirit sanctifying them to us. Further, the image of God himself is stamped on every creature, which only the believing eye can see. It is even revealed through mere vegetables, life, animals, understanding, and wisdom. And whatever of God is in a creature is most glorious. God that is in them has laid his command upon them to do us good (if we believe) and goodness is glorious.

The divine order in God's dispensations of outward things – first this, then that – as is best for our welfare is also glorious. He first provides for us the breast, then bread. He dispenses as the parent does clothes, fit for our age so they sit handsomely on our frame. Disorder is uncomely, but order is glorious. He does not give us everything at once to overwhelm us; nor the last thing first, or the first last.

2. There is a glory in spiritual gifts as knowledge, elocution, *etc.*, but in grace and graces there is more. The grace of God's favor clothes us with Christ's righteousness. This must necessarily be glorious, being the righteousness of God (2 Cor. 5). Consider how grim the sight of sin was before you saw the glory of Christ's robe of righteousness and how that if you do not see yourselves in Christ, clothed with his righteousness; you are a disgust to yourselves. But when you behold yourselves (and behold God in Christ's righteousness) you see your glory (1 Cor. 1). Christ is made to us righteousness, *etc.*, that he that glories may glory in the Lord. And then too, the graces of the saints are glorious. They are the spiritual creation of God (Eph. 2:10), the purchase of Christ's blood (Eph. 1:7-8), the breathings of the Spirit (John 20:22), the image of God in us (Eph. 4:24).

So that by all glories mentioned already, a saint is made most glorious within his own court or habitation. He dwells in Christ, glorious in his garments, glorious in his complexion; he is full of righteousness and holiness. Christ is most glorious, and as he is, so are we in this world (1 John 4:17).

3. Heaven is glorious, which is the platform of all our happiness. I need not argue this glory, but rather declare it. Here below we have a glory, but it is like the glory of the

moon and the night-shining of the stars, in comparison to heaven, which is as the glaring of diamonds, or sparkling of crystal, the gloss of gold at the sight of the noonday sun. In heaven every glory is heightened to a transcendency of luster. Our natural bodies shall glow brighter than the face of Moses, Stephen, or innocent Adam; namely, like the body of Christ (1 Cor. 15). Our reason and understanding shall be equal with, if not higher than, the intellectuals of the highest angels, since we are nearer in union with God through Christ than they. And as for our graces, every grace shall be raised to the highest perfection, for there in glory we will see God, either by the light of glory elevating the understanding with a supernatural strength to behold him or by the light of glory, elevating and strengthening the understanding to the highest pitch of apprehension to behold the divine essence. By our unspeakable union with Christ, we shall apprehend God as he apprehends him, to our utmost proportion.

In heaven the fountain of our happiness is *substantial glory*. Namely, God himself, perfecting our substances to the highest of our kind, along with the angels, full of superlative glorious qualities, will fill heaven with rays of both, and we will be perfected in all things to a glorious hue and luster. The flower-colored shining spring, the golden sea with morning beams, or the spangled starry heavens in a serene evening, are only shadows to this glory that we will know in heaven. Our communion there is like the most ravishing music, our sights all of admiration, and our thoughts seraphic raptures.

The fourth thing to be explained is the means, namely, Christ Jesus. God himself is able to supply all things, being infinitely rich and glorious. And naturally he is willing, as the chief good, to communicate his goodness to his creatures. But the way he has chosen to communicate himself to fallen man is through his son, Jesus Christ. God foreseeing what was wisdom and justice to himself, chose us in Christ. And now in time he communicates himself no other way but through Jesus Christ. He is fixed in, and shines through the orb of Christ Jesus (2 Cor. 4). He shines to us in the face of Christ Jesus. As there was no light to be communicated to the world but through the sun, the light of God is communicated to man solely through Christ.

1. Christ's incarnation is the fundamental insurance of our assurance that we are nearer to God than angels (Heb. 2), that he will be our Immanuel (Matt. 1) applied to our justification and salvation (Rom. 8). And so, he will do by us as he did by Christ, in all excellencies whereof we may be capable.

2. The formal perfecting act of the virtue of this incarnation to communicate himself to us is our actual union with Christ by the spirit.

3. Christ is the pattern to which we must in all things be conformed, by this making us akin to God's image. Christ therefore is called *the firstborn of every creature.*

This doctrine is useful for all those who stand afar off from Christ, who doubt whether to throw themselves into Christ's arms and fully trust themselves with him. "Come," says this doctrine, "come in, come near, own God in Christ, and rejoice in him as your own." With assurance of faith you can then say, "my God shall supply all my needs." More than anything else, learn to claim the Lord, to cry by faith, "You are mine," as Thomas declared, "my Lord and my God," and as Mary affirms, "my God and my Savior." As they did, you may rely on him. Even more so, for you see him not only born, but also crucified for you before your eyes (Gal. 3:1). That is the gospel, which continually implores us to receive Christ (2 Cor. 5). Why then do men not come to Christ Jesus, through whom God will be such a rich supply? If you are rich, you are not rich indeed if you have not closed with Christ in faith. If you are honorable, you are not rightly honorable unless you put on Christ. Come therefore, come to God in Christ. Hear those glorious invitations in Isaiah 55:1 to the end of the chapter, as well as Revelation 22:17. Turn to them, read them, consider them. They woo you emphatically to come to Christ. The promise is to you, for it is to all that the Lord shall call, to all that obey his call (Acts 2:39). He died for the ungodly (Rom. 5). And he came with the intent not to condemn the world, but that the world through him might be saved (John 3:17).

O therefore, close with Christ, throw yourselves into his arms. Let your heart say, "he is mine by faith, mine in hope; I love him, and I give myself to him. I will lie in his arms, lean on his heart, live in his heart of love. There I will expect all blessings from God." Close with God in Christ, for here in the text and within this doctrine he calls to you in the marketplace of wisdom, to, "come see what you lack, see what you need. Do you want riches, honor, comfort, any or all of these things? See what ye lack, then come buy, and buy without money," (Isa. 55:1, Rev. 22:27). And according to the text, he will supply all your needs. Do you lack a comfortable habitation? Psalm 90:1 says, "Lord thou hast been our dwelling place in all generations." Do you lack riches? Solomon tells you the blessing of the Lord makes rich. And Paul tells you that godliness is great gain. If we want to rule over all things, his power shall be your chambers to hide in (Isa. 26:20). His love shall be your bride chamber to rejoice in (Song of Songs 1:4). Do you lack peace? The apostle calls God, "the God of peace." And he promises in Isaiah 26:3, that "he will keep them in perfect peace, whose minds are stayed" on him. Do you lack friends? By faith Abraham was called the friend of God. God was a friend to him, for God justified him by faith (James 2:25). And by obedience that flows from faith we manifest we are Christ's friends (John 15:24). Do you lack wisdom about what to do and how to bear afflictions that perhaps arise from wants? If any man lack wisdom, let him ask it of God who gives it liberally (James 1:5).

If any man out of a willingness to follow Christ loses all, he shall find all, and will gain more than he lost in the end (Matt. 19:28-29).

Objection: For spiritual needs, God easily supplies them by immediate infusion. But how can he supply temporal needs where they do not exist?

Answer: God provided manna, but can he provide meat in the wilderness? He most assuredly can, (2 Kings 7:2). Doubting God is the language of our unbelieving hearts, as if we would provoke God to do nothing for us. Why, God has done and can do strange things, so that they seem to be done by creation. How wonderfully did he lead his people from Egypt into Canaan? And in his time he will turn Jerusalem into a city of joy. He will create peace.

Come therefore you disputers, listen to God, rely on him by faith, for he will be true, he must be true to you according to this text, to supply all your needs according to his riches in glory by Christ Jesus. Do you *feel* your need? Seek first the kingdom of God and his righteousness, and all other things shall be added to you. Go close with Christ, and then go to God and ask and have anything that you truly need that may do you good.

You may know whether your outward needs are a true and right need by what and how you ask them of God in prayer. That which you dare not ask boldly of God in prayer is not a true need. That which you dare not confidently beg of God in prayer is not a true need. And that way or manner or means of attaining something is not a true need if you cannot with a free heart petition God for his blessing on the same. When God has a mind to bend his ear, he will prepare the heart to pray (Psa. 10:17). Therefore, go to God by faith, address him by prayer in faith for a supply of whatever you *need*. Say here it is, here it is to be had, I will go no further than this door. Here I will stay and beg until I receive.

The devil tells us that he and his lifestyle will supply our need. So it was told the angels that fell as well as Adam. Evil spirits say, "the world will listen to us, and so they will supply all you ask. Simply come over to us, go our way, come plot in our plot, cooperate, and comply in our design, and we will make you happy men forever." These creatures with their beautiful looks will smile and promise much, and our own corrupt hearts, and carnal reasons will tell us many fairy tales. But all they can do is supply our senses with sensible things and leave our inward man to faint and fail; or they will supply our lusts with impure objects, which are worse than nothing and whose end is to poison and pain us to all degrees of misery. They say they will supply, but according to what? In stark contrast to the text, they will supply according to the abundance and baseness of evil that is in sin and the devil. But the voice of the text is life, the voice of God indeed. He will supply all your need according to the riches of his glory by Christ Jesus.

Those who own God in Christ can say, "my God by the blood of Christ, my God by the spirit of faith." These same men shall be able to say, "my God shall supply all my needs, mine and others who are believers, as Paul speaks in the text, for himself and other saints." God shall supply all widows, orphans, and prisoners with everything they have absolute need of, without fail.

First, we have absolute need of grace, for, "without faith it is impossible to please God," (Heb. 11). And God tells us we have need of patience (Heb. 10:36). Therefore, that same God must needs supply according to his promise. "He will pour out his Spirit," (Acts 2). He filled Christ with his fullness, so of that fullness we might receive (John 1:14).

Secondly, there is an absolute need for what is necessary for gracious behavior in all conditions. Hebrews 4:16 instructs us, "Let us come boldly unto the throne of grace, that we may obtain mercy and grace in time of need." And "my grace is sufficient for you, even in your wrestling with Satan," (2 Cor. 12, 1 Cor. 10:13). Therefore, this also God must supply.

Thirdly, that is of absolute necessity that is required for life while God has us on earth for his service. In this respect Christ said of outward things, "your heavenly father knows you have need of these things." Therefore, so much of food, of clothes, of liberty, of peace, *etc.*, as we need to act in accordance with God's mind, God must supply.

Fourthly, there is an absolute need that God should be glorified by us. He must attain his end. All things were made for his glory (Rev. 4:11). Therefore, whatever is needed for us to further God's glory, God must supply.

All these are necessary supplies. But sometimes God supplies superabundantly, "good measure pressed down, and running over," not only out of our necessity, but for our delight. And he will so supply our present need in some things that we can confidently speak from our experience regarding our future needs, as Paul says in the text, "my God shall supply all your needs." Paul also speaks in 1 Corinthians 1:10, "Who delivered us from so great a death, and does deliver; in whom we trust he will yet deliver." And again, in Romans 5:3, "tribulation works patience, patience experience, experience hope." Past mercies are the first fruits of the future.

And God suitably supplies whatever his saints need in this world. Hell, and the world endeavor to put the saints in a position of need. But the text says that *"God will supply all your need."* Hell, and the world labor to make his saints poor, scanty, and miserable; but the text says that "God will supply all your need *according to his riches."* Hell, and the world do nothing but render them contemptible. But the text says that "God will supply according to his riches *in glory."* Hell, and the world labor to divide the saints from Christ. But the text says, "God will supply them *by Christ Jesus."*

Objection: But how will God supply us?

Answer: Either ordinarily or extraordinarily, God is pleased to use means, but he is not tied to means, method, or manner of acting. When Moses was much with God on the mount he was able to fast for forty days. When Peter had a vision (Acts 10), he forgot his hunger. When Paul was caught up in a rapture, he did not know whether he was in the body or not, and therefore was unaware of any bodily needs. While Adam walked with God, he was unaware of his nakedness. No perplexities could hamper and seize Paul's spirit while he considered Christ's fullness, through whom he *can do all things* (Phil. 4:13). A word from Christ's mouth stills him in a great fight of temptations (2 Cor. 12). No matter what we face in the world, remember that Christ must reign (Psa. 2; Heb. 2). All the kings and rulers of the world will fall when God is ready to set up Christ as king in Jerusalem, including the antichrist (Dan. 2; Rev. 18). Christ's church must be established in glory (Rev. 21), and he will appoint his saints to rule (Rev. 20). These truths, I must say, will quiet our minds.

Objection: But my heart is still full of doubts.

Answer: Do you call God, "my God?" And do you have past experiences where he has supplied your needs? Then you may boldly say, as Paul did in the text, that "my God shall supply all my needs." The same God that makes any promise will give assurance that he will make good on his promise to all those who give serious consideration to it. In hopeful waiting upon God, a soul often has much communion with God. And in this communion, God makes memorable impressions on their spirits concerning assurance (Psa. 130:5-7). So that if all the world should tell them that they were waiting in vain, they would not be persuaded. Not only that, but there have also been some saints in times of great sufferings who have had an impression of prophesy made upon their spirits. The last martyr burned at the stake in Smithfield told his fellow believers that they should be of a good comfort, for he was persuaded he was the last that should suffer under Queen Mary; and so he was.

Question: When will God supply?

Answer: He will supply when his time is come, and he will not wait a minute longer than the time he has allotted; nor will he act a minute afore his predetermined time. But just at the very minute he is ready, he will do it (John 2). Christ's first miracle came while he was attending a wedding feast and the family ran out of wine. His mother, Mary, tells Christ about it, and he answers her that his hour had not yet come. But when those last sands ran through the hourglass of God's timing, he asked that the servants bring him pots of water, which he turned into wine. We can be assured that Christ will be punctual at the instant that it is right for him to do us good.

Objection: There are many great men and means to hinder those supplies which we need.

Answer: But what can prevent the God of the universe to do his will? Who can resist God when he impresses on great men's hearts, that they shall not hurt nor hinder? Both Laban and Esau came out in fury against Jacob, but God impressed them that they should not hurt him, and they became as tame and gentle as lambs. Plots have been made against us, as we said before, by great men. But God impressed them to not act, nor execute anything.

Objection: But I am full of unworthiness.

Answer: So it is that you are unworthy in yourself, but seeing it, and acknowledging it, is the way to remove it, so that it is not an impediment. Especially if you look from yourself to God's free mercy through Christ (Psa. 130:4), because the text says that "God will supply all your need according to his riches in glory by Christ Jesus."

Though you are unworthy, believe and trust in Christ who is worthy. He accepts us in him the beloved, (Eph. 1). O that men would not take up religion for the favor of great men, but so that they may experience true faith, hope, and communion with God. For to lie in God's heart will quiet the soul when all other helps are suspended.

Objection: I am in such a state and condition of afflictions, imprisonments, *etc.*, that are quite contrary to any probability that my wants or needs should be supplied.

Answer: In order to show his wisdom and power, and to exercise our faith, God often takes contrary courses to supply us with what we need. As it was in creation, before God made a beautiful, orderly, full-of-light world, he first created chaos engulfed in darkness. Likewise, in his providence, he often works contrary to what our minds can conceive. God sent Moses and Aaron into Egypt where his people were slaves, to free them and lead them to the promised land. But when Moses began entreating with pharaoh to let God's people go, things went worse for them.

To fulfill his purposes, sometimes God sends us into afflictions, and seems to hide himself, that we might pray, and believe, and hope, until he returns to help. And as for being imprisoned, the wise man would say that a free man is freer in prison than a fool is at large. This is most gloriously true spiritually, for if Christ has made us free, *we are free indeed.* It's a brave freedom to go to prison to be free in conscience. Joseph had to go through prison to be advanced in the kingdom. The Lord directed Jeremiah to the potter's house to teach him the lesson that he needed to learn about free grace, that God will have mercy, because he will. A prisoner condemned to be beheaded spoke these words while his head rested on the scaffold: "If there had been an easier way for me to go to heaven than this, I should have found it: but God would lead me this way rather than no other way there."

Objection: You have given many fair words, but they all seem to be nothing more than *opinions*.

Answer: Are these only notions which hold forth that which only God can give, namely, contentment? For God in Christ is the only true contentment. This is best observed when comparing a poor believer and a rich unbeliever with each other. The poor believer has much contentment, and the rich unbeliever, though he seems to have everything he wants, is not content. Is this a mere notion? "If he spared not his own son, how shall he not with him freely give us all things," (Rom. 8, Psa. 37). "I have been young and now am old, yet I never saw the righteous forsaken." Is God's intimate care for crows, sparrows and ravens mere notions? From this point our Savior argues: how much more will God take care of men that trust in him? Are those notions, that prove by experience to be real? A woman in these hard times having lost her estate found herself needing clothes for her children. So, she fell down before the Lord in prayer, "Lord this child needs a coat, and that child needs clothes. What shall I do? My eyes and hopes are upon you and look to you for help." And suddenly the Lord strangely provided for them.

"Come," said the husband to the wife, "if it is the will of God that this difficulty should be upon us, we will hire more help to attend, and settle into the affliction." And behold presently the Lord took away the affliction.

Therefore, I conclude, believe, pray, hope, and wait on God, and he shall (according to the infallible truth of this text) supply all your need according to his riches in glory, by Christ Jesus. Amen.

Part 2: God's Gracious Thoughts Towards Great Sinners

"But I know the thoughts I think towards you, says the Lord, thoughts of peace, and not of evil, to give you an expected end," (Jeremiah 29:11).

"The love of Christ passes knowledge," (Ephesians 3:19)

Nathanael Holmes, to the church in fellowship with him.

Dear brethren and sisters,

    My compassion for those among you whose hearts are now burdened and breaking put me on this discourse. Further, your unexpected requests have moved me to print it. For this reason, it was quickly compiled and ruggedly delivered, unpolished and untrimmed for public view of all abroad. But being desirous that you should have it sooner than later, I would rather deny myself of honor before denying you of any spiritual comfort I might be able to offer you, who am yours in the Lord by many strong obligations.

Nathanael Holmes
From my study in Mary Staynings.
December 2, 1646.

God's Gracious Thoughts Towards Great Sinners

Isaiah 55:8-9, "For my thoughts are not your thoughts, neither are your ways my ways, says the Lord. For as the heavens are higher than the earth, so are my ways higher than your ways, and my thoughts than your thoughts."

The first part of this chapter is a most glorious invitation to poor sinners to obtain free mercy (verse 1). This plea continues to the end of the 7th verse, where the Lord tells all who come to him that he will have mercy on them, and he will abundantly pardon. Or, translated nearer to the original Hebrew, it is expressed as, "he will multiply pardons." These verses clearly demonstrate the freeness, fullness, and faithfulness of God's glorious grace and favor, in order to counter all doubt and chase away all fears that lie in the hearts of hopeless sinners. Further, having removed their sins, God will also remove their judgments and change their sorrows into joys (verses 12-13). These verses are for the purpose of removing their doubts and fears.

It is as if the Lord is saying, "When I say, 'I will have mercy, and abounding, or multiplied pardoning mercy, you ought not doubt it, nor fear; for my thoughts are not your thoughts. For as the heavens are higher than the earth, so are my thoughts higher than your thoughts. For as the rain comes down from heaven," *etc.*

And then says the Lord, "your sins being done away means your judgments shall also be removed." Verses 12-13 say, "For you shall go out with joy," *etc.* You shall, by the effect of removing your sorrows, discern the cause, namely, the pardoning of your sins.

Out of them all, I chose this one doctrine for this discourse: the incomparable nature of God's gracious thoughts toward poor sinners which is above and beyond their own thoughts and is sufficient to stop the mouth of all objections and still the cries of all sadness and all miseries.

In terms of this rich doctrine, note that our miseries are twofold: afflictions and transgressions. Of the two, transgressions are much more painful. A confluence of all afflictions in and of themselves cannot sting as much as a single sin when God pricks the conscience with it. Paul's strong sexual desires stung him more than "his being killed all the day long," (Rom. 7:1-2). Afflictions whip the body; sin attacks the soul. As Solomon says, the spirit of a man may sustain his infirmities; but a wounded spirit who can bear (without God's grace)? (Prov. 18:14).

Also observe that in all these afflictions and sins, God's thoughts toward poor sinners are such as are incomparable and transcendent, above and beyond what we can think. 1. That is, we cannot think toward others as God thinks toward us. 2. Or, we are unable to conceive what those thoughts of God are toward us in our misery, just as he thinks them. Both meanings seem to be supported by the text. For the first, "I can," says the Lord, "show mercy wherever there is a sense of misery, though that misery did also provoke me by the sin of it, as it did grieve man with the affliction of it. For my thoughts are not your thoughts."

For the second meaning, "If there is abundance of sins bringing abundance of judgments, I can," (the Lord says) "abundantly pardon. For my thoughts are above your thoughts."

It is as if the Lord should say of the first, "Can you have such thoughts of mercy on misery as I can? Especially where you are provoked? Do you not usually repel violence with violence? Do you not usually render evil for evil? Are you not usually supporting the punitive way? Or if you pass by a few wrongs, can you pass by abundance? Do you not cry against multiple offences? You admonish, then punish. But I can think thoughts of mercy, contrary to all these," as has been shown in the text.

For the second, it is as if the Lord should say, "You can hardly think as I can think. For my thoughts are above yours. You are men, I am God. You corrupt, I purify. Do you see the disproportion of creatures, and of the heavens above the earth? Then note how high my thoughts are above yours. These are the thoughts I put forth to stop the mouth of all objections and still your sorrowing, fearing, complaining, and hopelessness."

"If you object to any crooked unworthy thing to disparage my thoughts, and so to prejudice yourselves in laying hold on my thoughts, let the answer be, my thoughts not as yours. Mine in substance are all good and right. As my words are, so are my thoughts (Psa. 19). No evil, no iniquity, no cruelty exists in my thoughts. If you think any, you bring it with you; you can find none in me." You go about to pervert the straight ways and thoughts of the Lord (Acts

13:10). But the Lord's thoughts are like himself; the Lord's thoughts and ways are equal, and yours are *unequal* (Ezek. 18:25).

It is as if the Lord should say, "whatever your thoughts are, if they are not just, good, holy, *etc.*, they are not mine. You may object; you may think your thoughts are good. But whatever thoughts do not tend to your salvation, tend to bring you toward me and this word of mine, those thoughts are not my thoughts," (Ezek. 18, 33).

If you object, in that you cannot imagine how I can have such thoughts of mercy to such sinners as you are, the answer is, as the heavens are distant and different from the earth, so are my thoughts above yours. The heavens are so above the earth, that the earth with all its cedars, mists, clouds, and fiery meteors cannot reach it; and neither can your thoughts in a rational way reach mine. As the heavens are greater, so are my thoughts (Eph. 3:17). As the heavens are larger than the earth, so are my thoughts like myself, infinite. As the heavens are more glorious than the earth, so are my thoughts than yours. As the heavens give light, so do my thoughts to yours. And as the heavens shine on the bad as well as good (Matt. 5:45), so do my thoughts on sinners as well as on saints.

If you object, saying that though these are effectual expressions in themselves, they are not able to do much, I will answer you this: "As the heavens draw up mists and pour them down as rain, so shall my word be that expresses my thoughts. And as the heavens that I created rain and carry the sun across the sky, as the seasons bring spring and harvest, then surely my thoughts and my words shall not be in vain. As the earth waits on the heavens for seed time, springtime, and harvest to come, my thoughts shall take hold of your thoughts and overcome them and transform them into mine. Your thoughts shall trust in my thoughts of truth. Your thoughts shall hope in my thoughts of mercy. Your thoughts shall rejoice in my thoughts of love. And your thoughts shall rest quietly in my thoughts of peace that all your sins are pardoned, and so your judgments shall be satisfied."

This is useful to cause us to consider God's thoughts, so far as we are able by enlightened reason, regarding, 1. How different in kind our thoughts are from God's thoughts. 2. How distant and short in degree our thoughts are below God's thoughts, when we set about to apprehend them. Both are in this text, (*cf.* Jer. 29:11).

As to the difference in kind, 1. Our thoughts cannot be first toward God in terms of our salvation. In other words, naturally our thoughts and imaginations are only evil continually (Gen. 6:5). We go astray as soon as we are born. So, God's thoughts are initial and precede our salvation. The psalmist says that, "he understands our thoughts afar off," or long before. Therefore, his thoughts precede ours. He makes the first motion toward our salvation (1 John 4:19). We love him because he loved us first; and therefore, his thoughts first move ours. His love first sounds forth, then our love responds. He first allures, then we are drawn. It is a mighty comfort that since his thoughts are first towards us, their graciousness must needs be free. Though we cannot glory in our thoughts, yet we may glory in this – that God's thoughts anticipate, prevent, and persuade our thoughts. God's thoughts are the original, ours are only the copy.

2. Our thoughts are not kind thoughts, sweet thoughts to others; we are self-lovers, which is the original sin of the world (see Adam). Do we think thoughts of love for our enemies? Do we seek them out that we might show them kindness? Would their misery make us sad or joyful? So uncharitable is our natural state that we rejoice in iniquity. But God's thoughts are all contrary to these.

3. Our thoughts are limited thoughts. We cannot pity or pardon (if we do either) much or many. But God's thoughts of mercy are abounding thoughts and multiplying thoughts, thoughts of abounding mercy, for he multiplies mercies and pardons. He shows mercy to thousands of generations (Exod. 20) as well as to thousands of sins of one soul. He heals backslidings (Hosea 14). And the psalmist speaks of a multitude of his mercies (Psa. 5:7, Psa. 100:7). Isaiah speaks of multitudes of his loving kindnesses (Isa. 63:7). And Jeremiah says there is no failing of his mercy, so we are not consumed. How much and how many evils did he pardon in Manasseh, Magdalen, and Saul? How many backslidings in Peter, and much more in Solomon? Even as true believers do not make an end of sinning, so God cannot make an end of pardoning. And as his pardoning removes our fear of sin, so it also removes our love of sin. His good will replaces our ill will (Rom. 7).

4. Our thoughts at best have much reluctance for good and typically much evil in them (Rom. 7). But God's

thoughts are all good, altogether pure and perfectly good. They concern our good and cure us of our evil (Jer. 29:11). "God is good, and does good," (Psa. 119).

5. Our thoughts, when they are not vile are vain (Jer. 4:14). But God's thoughts are great thoughts, touching the great things of our salvation.

6. Our thoughts focus on contentions with men and transgression against God (Isa. 55:7). But God's thoughts are of peace and reconciliation. This is affirmed in the text, as well as in Jeremiah 29:11. He is the God of all peace, and his thoughts are consistent with who he is.

7. Our thoughts are craving, begging thoughts. We consistently think of ways to get the upper hand over man by intreating him and gaining favor from God by praying. We are more in prayer than in praise. But God's thoughts are giving thoughts, bountiful thoughts, thoughts of giving before we ask, and giving so many times more than we dare ask. When they are despairing, he would be giving. "I am found of them that sought me not," (Isa. 65:1). God gave more to Paul than he thought on (Acts 9, 1 Tim. 1). Indeed, Solomon received more from God than he asked for. So, the promise is to "seek first the kingdom of God." We often ask to believe, but he gives more (Phil. 1:29). We often ask for strength to overcome some sin, but God gives us strength to overcome many other sins as well. It is true, that it is a more blessed thing to give than to receive, for God blessed forevermore gives. And even when we continue asking, God is *never* weary of giving. Many more particulars might be

given of the different kinds of our thoughts from God's, but these are enough to enlarge our meditation.

8. When we refocus our thoughts to understand the incomparable thoughts of God towards us, our ability falls infinitely short of comprehending them as we should. Thus, "My thoughts are above your thoughts."

Further, God's thoughts regard such matters as mercy, goodness, and pardoning in measures beyond our ability to grasp as follows:

1. They are infinite. Psalm 92:5 says, "O Lord, how great are thy works, thy thoughts are very deep," as in the "deep things of God," (1 Cor. 2:10). They must be so in order to shelter us from the "depths of Satan," his evil schemes and temptations (Rev. 2:24). God's understanding is infinite, (Psa. 147:5). In Romans 11:33, the apostle makes a heavenly exclamation, "O the depth of the riches both of the wisdom and knowledge of God, how unsearchable are his judgments, and his ways past finding out!" God has thoughts of mercy for millions of sinners, and therefore certainly enough for *all* the sins of *one* sinner.

2. They are continual. His thoughts of mercy, goodness, and pardon continue without interruption. They have no beginning nor ending, and no breaking off in the middle (Eph. 1; Psa. 89).

3. They are certain, firm and established. As stated in the text, "the sure mercies of David," that is, what is promised to David is fulfilled in Christ, the son of David. As sure as Christ is in our nature, we are one with him by faith. Christ is the great pledge, or witness, of God's merciful

thoughts toward us poor sinners. Though we are unlovely in ourselves, yet we are acceptable and well-pleasing to God in Christ (Matt. 3; Eph. 1:3).

4. They are immutable, both in kind and degree. They cannot be otherwise, or less than they have ever been (2 Tim. 2:19). And James says, "with him is no shadow of change." Yes, God in Christ is the same yesterday, today and forever (Heb. 13).

5. They are intuitive. God thinks all his thoughts at once. As a man's eye sees all it sees at that look, in one twinkling of an eye God sees all that was, is, and will be at once in absolute detail. He does not need any rational or intellectual discourse to go from one thing to another in his thoughts. He simply can and does comprehend all at once.

Considering these and similar properties of God's thoughts, we fall completely short of apprehending God's thoughts. As such, we move to doubting, because in opposition ...

1. To the infinite nature of God thoughts, our thoughts are finite. We see with a limited eye. Not even the sun can light all the world at once, so how much farther do our finite thoughts fall short of God's infinite thoughts.

2. To the continuity of God's thoughts, ours are interrupted, broken off oftentimes in the middle. Many by-thoughts intervene, disturb, and dissipate our most serious thoughts, when we attempt to apprehend God's thoughts or anything that is good.

3. To the certainty of his thoughts, our thoughts are most uncertain. Sometimes they are more conjectures than

resolves, more opinions than judgments, more disputing than determination. And as the inability of our eye to behold the fixed stars at such a distance makes us think they twinkle, our uncertainty in thinking makes us think God's thoughts are uncertain, when in reality it is the uncertainty and variability of our own thoughts.

4. To the immutability of God's thoughts, which stands in opposition to the mutability of own our thoughts. Sometimes they are on God, and sometimes they are on the creature instead. And when it is on God, it is sometimes stronger, sometimes weaker, sometimes almost nothing. Sometimes they catch one thing, and let that go, and then catch another, and so lose the series, method, and dependence of things necessary to find out the excellency of God's thoughts.

5. The intuitive nature of God's thoughts stand in opposition to the informality of our thoughts. Our reason is imperfect, and our knowledge is partial. We struggle to understand ordinary things, much less those subjects that are more extraordinary and supernatural. We cannot always by the compass of reason comprehend even some natural things; how then can we expect to reach God's intuitive thoughts?

Now therefore says the Lord in the text, when you hear me speak of such high things as are here mentioned, as "I will abundantly pardon," *etc.*, you wonder at them, but do not doubt them or dispute them, for, "my thoughts are known to me," (Jer. 29:11). They are not so base and low as yours, but far above (Isa. 55). They are as high above your thoughts as the heavens are above the earth.

Both our text here and Jeremiah 29:11 hold forth the following particulars:

1. No man nor angel can tell my thoughts as well as I can. Flesh and blood could not reveal to Peter the things of Christ (Matt. 16:17). And in 1 Corinthians 2, "the natural man receives not the things of God, because they are spiritually discerned. Nor can your spiritual minds comprehend the fullness of these things, for you know only in part," (1 Cor. 13). As the nations do not know my thoughts, nor understand my counsel concerning you, so you may labor to know them, but still they will pass your knowledge (Micah 4:12; Eph. 3:19). The loving thoughts of my heart are better felt than understood, for I shed my love into your hearts (Rom. 5).

2. I know all my own thoughts perfectly; how high they may be, I comprehend them all. They are all distinctly written in my heart, and I know every one of them to a tittle.

3. I acknowledge my thoughts to be high thoughts of love, mercy, *etc.* I do not desire to keep them to myself, but choose to explain them to you, though you cannot reach to the height of them. I make them legible to your eyes in my book. I make them frequently sound in your ears in the ministry of my word, and I give you a representation of them in the sacraments to many of your senses. Though you cannot comprehend them fully as they are infinite in every way, yet you may admire them as perfectly infinite and incomprehensible.

Part 2: God's Gracious Thoughts Towards Great Sinners

4. Though your thoughts have many objections against my thoughts, yet I know my thoughts will answer all the objections of your thoughts. Dispute and try.

It may be that you poor sinners will say you have had such deep apprehensions of your sins, and such long inner conflicts about them, that you think you shall never know what a good day feels like ever again.

But (based on these texts), my thoughts toward you are thoughts of mercy and of multiplying pardons that are above your comprehension. My thoughts toward you are thoughts of peace; I think peace toward you, as I am the God of peace. Your thoughts cannot imagine great things, because your thoughts are not like my thoughts.

It may be that you will object again, saying that you think my thoughts toward you are not such thoughts of mercy because my hand has been upon you to afflict you. And perhaps the affliction or its pain has not yet left you. Therefore, you think my thoughts toward you are severe. But my thoughts are as these texts declare.

You can be angry, even irreconcilably angry with men because flesh and blood are prone to be unmerciful and unforgiving. But my thoughts are not such; for my thoughts cannot be like yours, they must be better, and above yours, or they cannot be my thoughts. I tell you plainly in such texts as Isaiah 55, "Let him that has nothing come and buy," (verse 1). That "there is a time when I will be found," (verse 6). And the present time when I offer grace and favor is the accepted time (2 Cor. 6:2). Christ Jesus, who was made sin for us, hears sinners. So, my thoughts of anger toward sin are but for a time, but my thoughts of mercy are everlasting (Psa. 30:5, 89:28). I have sworn not to be angry with sinners forever but have sworn to have mercy. Though I afflict my people, yet I have thoughts of peace to them at last (Jer. 29:11). And while I am afflicting them, I have thoughts of love (Heb. 12). Therefore, the Lord says, do not be weary of the Lord's chastisement (Prov. 3:11-12), but do as Isaiah 8:17 says, "I will wait upon the Lord, and I will look for him."

3. It may be that you poor sinners will object that your thoughts are not able to bear your sorrows of sins and afflictions. Therefore, you would have them removed. Yet I, the Lord, have all manner and measure of mercies to take away the burden of your affliction. And I have employed my pardoning mercy for you (Jer. 29:12).

4. It may be that you believe your perplexities and miseries have been so many and so long that you can never again have the presence and comfort of God. But the Lord says in our text that "I have abundance of mercy for you, multiplied mercy; yes, so much as your thoughts cannot reach to. And it shall satisfy you, as the rain does the earth; and not only you shall rejoice, but the world shall seem before you to sing and to be full of joy."

5. And yet maybe some of you have waited a long while for God's peace and joy, without having yet attained it. But remember that his thoughts are not as our thoughts. Rather, just as the heavens are above the earth and in due time they water it, you shall have your expectation. Hope is not ashamed at the last, nor while it waits, because the love of God is shed abroad in our hearts (Hab. 2:3-4).

By meditating on God's incomparable thoughts, we can see how they prevent all objections and cause us to exercise our faith. Because where our best thoughts fall short, there the faith that Christ has given us may ascend.

As we give greater consideration to how high God's thoughts are above our own, we see more clearly God's grace and favor to sinners. We see that his thoughts arise from the sweet, good, and unspeakable excellency of his nature, "Thou art good, and thou do good." Out of the evil nature of man proceeds all evil thoughts, adulteries, murders, thefts, *etc.* There was no good in us when God first thought of us to move him to think on us; for either he looked on us as nothing, or as most sinful, unworthy beings. Yet nothing could hinder him from his gracious thoughts towards us. As it is said, he will have mercy on whom he will have mercy. He will think what he will think of grace and favor to poor sinners; nothing can help, and nothing shall hinder him. As God cannot be otherwise in his nature than he is, so he cannot be otherwise in his gracious thoughts than what he will think.

Objection: But God has a pure nature, and a just nature, *etc.* And therefore, by the same proportion must arise thoughts of hating sin and punishing unrighteousness, with which by nature we abound.

Answer: This does not contradict God's thoughts of grace and favor to grievous sinners, because God is pure and just from all eternity, foreseeing all things, he continues with those thoughts of grace and favor.

Also, God is pleased to propose to us his justice conditionally, upon our obstinacy against mercy. But he also holds forth his offer of mercy absolutely, without any condition of ours (Isa. 55:1, 43:25, Rev. 22:17).

3. God is pleased to signify to us that he loves to have his mercy rejoice over his justice (James 2:13). Grace *glories*. It is the glory of God's mercy that it prevents judgment. In that God hates sin, and because of his just nature must punish it, he has provided a Savior to remove the guilt and filth of sin (1 Cor. 1). Christ took our nature on himself, sanctifying it, and making atonement by it to be sin for us, that we might be made the righteousness of God. On him he laid the iniquities of us all (Isa. 53). And on us he laid the righteousness of God (2 Cor. 5). The righteousness of God, good enough to be acceptable to himself and great enough being infinite, to appease him for the finite unrighteousness of man.

4. And lastly, God loves to dignify the second Adam above the first (Rom. 5; 1 Cor. 15). Where sin abounded, grace did much more abound. And as sin has reigned to death, so might grace reign through righteousness to eternal life by Jesus Christ our Lord. By which it appears that as before, sin did reign over us, so now God's gracious favor through Christ's righteousness should reign over our sins. And that the benefit might be imparted to poor sinners abounding with sin, God made his grace much more abound.

Exercise faith at the birth of these thoughts of mercy; namely, that as they are conceived from God's most excellent sweet nature, so they bring forth a gracious purpose or choosing (Rom. 8:29). Whom he did foreknow (out of those thoughts of mercy that were conceived in his sweet nature) he did predestinate and appoint to be made conformable to his son, Christ Jesus. As Ephesians 1:3-5 states, "He hath blessed us with all spiritual blessings in heavenly places in Christ. According as he has chosen us in him before the foundation of the world, having predestined us to the adoption of children by Jesus Christ to himself, according to the good pleasure of his will." It is evident here that the good will of God gives rise to predestination; and predestination gives rise to purpose. Those purposes of God are free and unconstrained and arise out of his own free nature and good will. Ephesians 1:11 says, "In whom (that is in Christ) we have obtained an inheritance, being predestined according to the purpose of him that worketh all things according to the counsel of his own will." Observe that he does not say, "according to the counsel of his understanding." As if he would know, find, and consider something in us. But according to the counsel of his own will. His good will and sweet inclination to poor sinners is that which puts forth these thoughts of grace and favor. So that as in Isaiah 43:25, he assures us that as he can love himself, so he can blot out sins. He cannot be of another nature but to bring good will to men. He is of a sweet and merciful disposition, so he provides salvation to poor and needy sinners.

2. These purposes of favor are unchangeable. As 2 Tim. 2:19 states, "the foundation of God stands sure, having

this seal, the Lord knows who are his." So, against all fears of change, this becomes an assurance, that whom he loves, he loves to the end (John 13:1). With him, James says, is *no shadow* of changing. Therefore, God is unmovable from his purposes of mercy by anything in us or from us.

Objection: But in God's purpose and predestination lies also his reprobation, and that breeds doubt and fear.

Answer: It is true that while God elects some, he passes by others. But this passing by, or non-election, is when God in his foreknowledge knows that a man will sin obstinately and perpetually against the means of grace offered to him. For this reason, God pre-condemns him. God's election of his own is a free gift and not as a result of any imperfect deserving of our own. Our salvation is solely based on the gift and power of God's goodness, but reprobation is brought on by sin, since we freely and fully sin of ourselves. A magistrate may reward a subject freely when they have done some good for their government, even though the good deed is a sufficient reward of itself, as virtue is an outward honor among civil, honest men. But the magistrate cannot with any justice condemn or punish any subject, or purpose to do so, without some evidence of that man's transgressing. By the same proportion, with infinitely more exactness, God purposes and elects to salvation freely, but does not reprobate any to condemnation without sure evidence that the same will sin unrepentantly against the means of grace (2 Chron. 36:11-16; Prov. 29:1).

But you will say that God's passing by those that are not elected means that they cannot be saved. We answer that the matter rests in God's infallibility, for he cannot be deceived. He does not place constraints on men that force them to sin. As the angels who were full of glory voluntarily sinned in heaven, and Adam who was created sinless and full of glory freely sinned in paradise, so do we now in the world. God does not predestine certain men to be damned because they are sure to sin, *for we all are*. He does so because he knows before the beginning of time those that will reject grace in their lifetime. And yet, notwithstanding his eternal thoughts of pre-damnation, he allows every man sufficient outward means and inward light to understand those means before he damns them eternally to hell. (2 Chron. 36; Prov. 29).

Our second answer is this, that predestination is a long golden chain, impregnable, inseparable, unbreakable. (Rom. 8:29-30, Eph. 1:3-12, 2 Tim. 2:19). If we see but the least and last link fastened to our hearts in order to sanctify us so that we may sincerely desire and endeavor to depart from iniquity, you may be sure that the other end of the chain is fastened to God's heart by eternal election.

Our third answer is to consider those passages like Romans 8 and Ephesians 1 where God's decrees relate first to Christ and then pass through him, that as we look on Christ to receive him or refuse him, so we may conclude it will be so with our predestination.

Regarding the birth, existence, and characteristics of God's thoughts, let's now consider how they come to be toward us and how they are manifested to us.

1. God's thoughts delightfully reflect on themselves; God takes a great deal of pleasure in his own gracious thoughts to poor sinners. In Deuteronomy 30:9, it is said that "God delights to do us good." And Micah 7:18, "Who is a God like thee, that pardons iniquity, and passes by transgression? He keeps not his anger forever, because he delights in mercy." Though mercy seems most to concern us, yet God is joyed in his own thoughts of mercy. We may be sad in the best thoughts we think for some mixture of sin or vanity in them, but God's thoughts are excellent like himself, so much so that he rejoices in them as in himself.

2. These thoughts delight in minding the good of poor sinners, and so consequently he takes delight that sinners should be the better for them (Deut. 30:9, Micah 7:18). The precious stones inscribed with the names of the 12 tribes of Israel that Aaron, the high priest, wore in his breastplate signify how Christ carries sinners in the thoughts and affections of his heart.

3. They are compassionate thoughts toward a poor sinner grieved over his sin. As Jeremiah 31:18 states, "I have surely heard Ephraim bemoaning himself thus; Thou hast chastised me, and I was chastised, as a bullock unaccustomed to the yoke: turn thou me, and I shall be turned; for thou art the Lord my God. Surely after that I was turned, I repented; and after that I was instructed, I smote upon my thigh: I was ashamed, yea, even confounded, because I did bear the reproach of my youth. Is Ephraim my dear son? is he a pleasant child? for since I spoke against him, I do earnestly remember him still: therefore my bowels are

troubled for him; I will surely have mercy upon him, saith the Lord." What a comforting place! God first puts these repenting thoughts into a poor sinner's heart, and then his heart melts with compassionate thoughts of mercy, resolving to show kindness to them.

4. They are patient opportunity-waiting thoughts, to do a poor distressed soul good. Isaiah 30:18 says, "And therefore will the Lord wait that he may be gracious unto you, and therefore will he be exalted to have mercy on you." For the Lord is a God of judgment [*equity or uprightness*]; blessed are all they that wait for him." The Lord declares himself to be good, full of thoughts to do some worthy work, to show some notable kindness, who stands observing and meditating when and how he may use the best opportunity to do it. He sets himself like a general in some high place, to view when he may step in to rescue and relieve those that are in danger and distress. God is thinking kind thoughts to us when he is not acting. And he will not wait one minute too long to show us mercy, when his time is come.

5. His thoughts are tender, caring thoughts, for the meek and broken heart. As Isaiah 66:2 says, "But to this man will I look, even to him that is of a poor and a contrite heart, and trembles at my word." God will not only look on such a one to have thoughts of pity; but he will look in order that he may bind his wounds. The poor that is despised of the world God will look to and shall be blessed in his thoughts (Matt. 5, Luke 4:18). In this is assurance that the meek are high in God's thoughts.

6. To prevent sin from withholding good things from us, God tells us that his thoughts are sin-surpassing thoughts, super-abounding above all sins. Many poor sinners cannot get their thoughts above their sins; their sins master their thoughts. But God's thoughts super-abound above and beyond all our sin and unworthiness. As Romans 5:20 states, "Where sin abounded, grace did much more abound." And 1 Timothy 1:14, "And the grace of our Lord was exceeding abundant..." or as it is in the Greek, *super-abounded.*

7. And lastly, the thoughts of God are always for them that love him. Romans 8:28, "And we know that all things work together for good to them that love him." How does the apostle prove this? From God's thoughts! See verse 29, *etc.*, "whom he foreknew, these he predestined to be confirmed to the image of his son." God's plot is none other than this, that the poor sinner that loves him shall fare no worse (according to his measure) than his son Christ Jesus. We are apt to think we shall be made miserable; but Christ is designed in God's thoughts to be the platform and forerunner of our condition. We are apt to think that the devil, sin, the world, and our own hearts conspire together for our ruin. But God's thoughts are that all, even all shall work together, cooperate, and combine together for our good. Whatever the evils of hell, Satan, and the world may intend, God's thoughts have plotted to bend all to this. And further, whom God foreknew, those he predestined, and whom he predestined, those he called, whom he called,

those he justifies, whom he justifies, those he glorifies. Nothing can intervene, invert, or subvert this order.

The third use is to perform our duty to this mercy.

1. To forsake our own thoughts (verse 7). That is, we are not to believe our own thoughts if they oppose in the least God's thoughts.

2. To be sure to think high enough and large enough of God's thoughts of favor. You know how great your sins are. But be sure to remember that your sins are finite, and God's thoughts of mercy toward you are infinite.

3. To draw near to, to invoke and seek the God of mercy in the time of his offer of mercy (verse 6, 2 Cor. 6:2).

4. To wait for the dispensations and manifestations of the acts of God's thoughts of mercy, as the earth waits expectantly on the heavens for rain (verse 10).

5. To look to God to make the expressions of the thoughts of your heart and make impressions upon them, as God makes it rain on the earth (verse 10).

6. And lastly, to take heed in the meantime of abusing mercy (verse 7).

Part 3:
God's Gracious Expressions

God's Gracious Expressions Engaging Himself with Those that Accept His Grace

"Blessed be God, even the Father of our Lord Jesus Christ, the Father of mercies, and the God of all comfort; who comforts us in all our tribulation, that we may be able to comfort them which are in any trouble, by the comfort wherewith we ourselves are comforted of God," (2 Cor. 1:3-4)

These words were spoken by the apostle to the saints at the church at Corinth, "Know ye not that the unrighteous shall not inherit the kingdom of God? Be not deceived: neither fornicators, nor idolaters, nor adulterers, nor effeminate, nor abusers of themselves with mankind, nor thieves, nor covetous, nor drunkards, nor revilers, nor extortioners, shall inherit the kingdom of God. And such were some of you: but ye are washed, but ye are sanctified, but ye are justified in the name of the Lord Jesus, and by the Spirit of our God," (1 Cor. 6:9).

These believers in Corinth had accepted God's gracious favor offered in Christ (though many of them very weakly, *cf.* 1 Cor. 3). And so now the apostle speaks to them as to saints, and members of the church at Corinth, "The God of all comfort, who comforts us to the end." Paul and Timothy identified themselves with the saints at Corinth who had received grace and favor, and here in the text demonstrates the assurance of this gift that God had given them through Christ: "Blessed be God, even the father of our Lord Jesus Christ who comforts us..." God is engaged with his people by many engagements to be to them all comfort.

Here are two general points to be explained: 1. The comfort that God is to his people. 2. The engagements upon God to be this comfort.

Regarding the first, comfort is from God. He is said in the text to be the God of comfort. Satan is the god of this world, the prince and power of the air, and the prince of darkness. He is called the accuser, the tempter, the wicked one, being the cause at least in part of all mischief and misery. On the contrary, God is the God of all comfort. Again, the world is said by John to be a world of wickedness and by Solomon to be vanity and vexation of spirit, and by the saints a wilderness (Song of Songs 3:6) in which is nothing but lack and desolation. In contrast, God is the God of all comfort. Death is said to be the king of terrors (Job 18:14), a thick darkness upon all the glory of men's worldly enjoyments. Yet God is the God of all comfort. A king may be called by great titles, invested with great power, clothed with great honor, surrounded by great wealth and all manner of prosperity able to make his queen, his children, his allies, favorites, *etc.*, outwardly happy.

And yet, above all, God is the God of all comfort. God in Christ is the king of kings and Lord of Lords, the only potentate, meaning that whatever comforts kings and princes may seem to have or hold forth to men, they had them from the king of kings, who has infinitely more to give than all the kings of the earth put together; and to give them more effectively and blessedly. For God is not only the administrator and dispenser of comfort, but the creator of comfort. He creates peace, he creates joy. So much so that a glimpse of his face, one beam of his countenance is heaven on earth, just as his presence is the glory of heaven.

Secondly, to tell you what comfort is of God, two things must be explained.

1) The quantity of the comfort that is from God, and, 2) The quality of the comfort that is from God.

Regarding the quantity of this comfort: 1. In number, the comforts from God are *plural;* they are many. God is merciful, but his mercy is in the plural and not in the singular. God knows we have many miseries, so he balances it with his many mercies. In Isaiah 55 he speaks of multiplying pardons because of our much sinning; and of loving kindnesses in the psalms because of our many wants; so here of mercies, because of our many miseries.

2. In kind, great is the quantity of comfort from God. God is the God of all kinds of comfort. If there is any comfort in husband, wife, friend, or child, it is because the image or impress of God is there. If there is any comfort in an ordinance, it is because God is present in it. If there is any comfort in creatures, it is because it comes from God, and leads us to God.

As there is more comfort in a friend oftentimes than in his gift, and we delight in giving a treasure to our friend instead of keeping it, so there is more joy in God and in serving him than in all we receive from him. As the sun is the origin of all natural light, so God is the origin of all comfort.

3. In degrees, great is the quantity of comfort that is from God. The first and lowest degree of his comfort is effective comfort. Though we suffer tribulation, a worse degree of affliction, yet God comforts us in all of this. As the threshing beats the wheat out of the chaff and makes it brighter, God desires to be glorified in our tribulation (Rom. 5). As the sufferings of Christ abound in us, so our consolation also abounds by Christ. As the psalmist says in Psalm 94:19, "In the multitude of my thoughts (*that is of sorrow*) within me, thy comforts delight my soul." Afflictions are sometimes the very reason for our rejoicing. As Matthew 10 notes, "When they persecute you for my name's sake, rejoice and be exceeding glad, for great is your reward." And in Acts, the apostles went away rejoicing from the council, that they were counted worthy to suffer for the name of Christ. Sometimes afflictions drive us nearer to God in prayer; and generally speaking, God is closest to his saints when he chastises us. As Psalm 94:12 says, "Blessed is the man whom thou dost afflict, and teach out of thy law." And James 1:2 says, "Count it all joy when you fall into diverse temptations." It is no small comfort, that God's beams pierce through the thick dark cloud of our sorrows, and his influence soaks through a world of trouble, to bring comfort, joy in sorrows, and life in death. Our comforts shall be greater through Christ than our sufferings can ever be for him, besides all that is to come. God is so effective in his comforting that he will comfort whom he will comfort. The

world may count it a reproach to be afflicted and persecuted; yet the Spirit of his glory and the comfort of the Father shall be ours in all tribulation. God comforts on the mount of temptation as well as in the valley of inward dejections. He comforts under the rod as Paul and the apostles were, in the stocks, in the lion's den, and in the fiery oven (Heb. 11). God gives us many graces against the body of sin and an army of comforts against all other discomforts. God is omnipotent in comforting, as well as in creating and preserving.

But secondly, and higher, this comfort from God is an understood and recognized comfort. We shall not only have comfort at times and not know it (Psa. 22), but we shall be comforted, and know we are comforted. Christ gave us his spirit that we may know the things that are given us of God (1 Cor. 2:12; Eph. 3; Rom. 5). He will cause us to feel it. He will shed it into our hearts. As we feel the comfort of the sun when we cannot behold its brightness, so it is in the knowledge of God's love.

Thirdly, and yet higher, it is often a redundant, super-abounding comfort. It shall be not only good measure pressed down for our use but running over for other's refreshment. We shall be able to comfort others because our comfort shall not only fill our banks of desires but float to the valley of saints round about us, as the widow's oil and meal fed her and the prophet too. As God comforted Christ in his sufferings, so he comforts us in ours (Heb. 5:7-9). And as we receive comfort from Christ, we can comfort one another. We shall light one another's candle while keeping plenty of light for our own.

Fourthly, and still higher, it is experiential comfort. We shall not only communicate our comforts to others, but we shall be able to share our experiences of comfort with the saints, how that in a time of distress we were supported. Those who do not know the consolations of God, consider them as nothing (Job 15:11). But we know what they are by our experiences.

Fifthly, and higher still, it is a strong and lasting comfort. It does not grow weak by pouring it out of one heart into another. But the same comfort that comforted us, comforts others. The same plaster heals many sores. This heavenly comfort is as good at last as it was at first. Simply consider that the same word, Spirit, and ordinances have comforted thousands for these 4000 years.

And lastly, God often sends so much comfort that it makes the soul magnify and bless God for it. God will not only give us comfort to live, but to joy in him, as the sun shines not only to make the plants grow but also to blossom. So, God hatches up comfort to the blossoming of *joy*. As flowers are the joy of plants, so joy is the blossom of our graces. As the psalmist said, in God we make our boast all day long. God will sweetly touch the heart-strings with the finger of his spirit, not only to make them sound with comfort, but to resound and echo praise. The world shall hear of the comfort that Moses, Deborah, Hannah, David, Elizabeth, Mary, Paul, Silas, and others received. God will delight his ear with his own music. He will put joy and gladness into the heart until it praise him.

In this way, the quantity of comfort shall be like the manna. He that gathered little had no further need, and he that gathered much had no extra.

Secondly, for the quality of comfort, it is the comfort that is of God. And God's comfort is like himself. The world's comfort is a lying comfort. The devil's comfort is a damnable flattering comfort. The best comfort from things on earth are mixed, if not muddled. But the comfort that is from God is like God in that it is pure and spiritual, it reaches to the soul and spirit of a man. A dram of this powder of pearl, Christ's comfort, is of more value than a hundred pounds of earthly comforts. One look of Christ at Peter makes him mourn that he didn't love Christ more. One glimpse of the transfiguration of Christ wraps up the three disciples and transports them into the third heaven. It makes the disciples despise all that is of the world. A word of this from Christ to Paul during his afflictions stilled him. A glance of God on Moses makes him glorious. Regarding other comforts, "in the midst of laughter the heart is sad," but this comfort makes the heart glad and adds no sorrow.

Next, we look at God's engagement of himself to comfort his own. We will note both the matter and the method of setting down these engagements here.

1. He is God, which means he is the chief good, the greater good in anything. God cannot be God without being good. He cannot be the greatest good, without communicating his goodness. From all eternity, God

secured in his thoughts his desire and plan to do us good. He conceived in himself the model of our being, and wellbeing. He designed two worlds for us – the one below for our natural bodies, another of glory in the world to come, for spiritual soul and body jointly. In this world we enjoy him because he communicates himself to us. He communicates that he is good. As in Psalm 119, "Thou art good, and do good." It is the impression of God's goodness upon all creation – sun, sea, elements, *etc.* – that makes them communicate comfort to man. How much more does God who is infinitely good communicate his comfort, because, as the text said, he is the God of comfort who shares his goodness. 2. And because he communicates that comfort to us, he will cease to communicate his comfort when he ceases to be God, and not before.

But are not the saints in need of comfort when they cry for it? To be sure, but even then they have a degree of saving comfort, else they would despair. It is of some comfort that they turn to God in prayer to get more, as the psalmist did in Psalm 22:1. For even while he cried for God's presence, he had this comfort, that he was *his* God.

2. He is the Father of our Lord Jesus Christ, the last man (as the apostle calls him in 1 Cor. 15). This second Adam is the everlasting Father to all believers (Isa. 9). As Christ is the representative of us all that believe, so God is our father in and through Christ, being Christ's father. Therefore, it is said, consider yourselves as being in him (Rom. 6:11). We are accepted in him (Eph. 1:6), and co-heirs with him (Rom. 8). God comforts Christ as he is the Father of Christ (Heb. 5),

so God comforts us as younger brethren (Heb. 2) and as members of his body (Eph. 4). This union between Christ and us is close and intimate (John 14:20, 17:22). Therefore, we may boldly say that as long as God comforts Christ, he must also comfort us that believe in Christ. If God maintains his Son's titles, (Lord, Jesus, Christ), then he must comfort us through him. He must defend and succor us under his Lord-ship, save us under his Jesus-ship, and anoint us spiritually with the spirit, by his Christ-ship.

Also, Christ's body now in heaven is an earnest that we shall be there too (John 14:2-3). Can any relation be more tender than that of a father? Can any son be dearer to God than Christ? Can any be nearer to Christ than we who believe, for we are joined to the Lord, and made one with his spirit? It must follow then, that because God has infinite love for Christ, he must also to us, as we are in him. He has no other to love as his children, and he has none else to bestow all his great estate upon.

Regarding engagement, God is the Father of mercies. Or as it is in the Greek, he is the "father of bowels of mercies." He is not only the author of mercies, but the Father of mercies; he gives all his gifts with a paternal affection.

By how many titles does our tenure of mercies hold good? One is that we are servants to God and to his Christ. We are also espoused to Christ as his bride (Hosea 2). We are God's children, and Christ's brethren. Further, God is the Father of mercies, who pities us as a Father does the child (Psa. 103). He bears with us, as a Father does a weak child that serves him as he can (Malachi 3:18). And he is the Father of mercies (plural, *i.e.,* "store of mercies"). God is not just the Father of Christ alone; all believers are included in him. And so he cannot be the Father of one mercy only, but of many, to have some for all, yes, many for everyone. He that is rich in mercies cannot leave his children poor.

4. Engagement. The God of all comfort defines what God is to us. The Lord God Jehovah is merciful, gracious, long-suffering, abundant in goodness, *etc.* (Exod. 34). So that this comforting of him to us is one of the jewels in his crown, and in this way God maintains his sovereignty. How shall he be said to be God, that is infinite good, if he is not full of comfort abounding toward us? And how can he be a God of all comfort if his people shall have none?

2. For the method of these engagements, in a word; the God of this comfort removes impediments that might hinder us. Believers who seek to acquire worldly goods do so with great dissatisfaction and disappointment (Eccl. 2:1-12). King Solomon had the best of all creature comforts, and yet he could find nothing but vanity and vexation in them all. Reading is a high and intellectual delight, and is therefore, for a while, a pleasure to the mind. But unless God comes in, reading for reading's sake compromises the understanding and does nothing to build the spirit (Eccl. 12:12). Music is pleasant to the ear, but unless God comes in to cheer the heart, it is nauseous to a man (Psa. 137). Odors are pleasant to the smell, but unless God blesses with health, they suffocate that sense, and cause fainting. Food is

pleasant to the taste; but unless God gives it his blessing, it upsets the stomach.

Solomon says that even in the midst of laughter, in all creature enjoyments that exclude God the heart is sad. Authority brings more tyranny than reformation. Honor tends to more arrogance than usefulness, wine makes mad more than it makes merry. And so it may be said of comfort, that even if all the world were called upon to provide it, without God it cannot. The sea answers, it is not in me. I am a devourer and make many a sea merchant sad. The heavens answer, it is not in me. For unless God help me, I cause barrenness (Hosea 2). And the sons of men confess (if they will speak the truth) that without God they are as Job's friends, *miserable comforters*. They can see one miserable, and say this and that, but without the benefits of God, they cannot comfort. One man is contented with a little. Why? God is there. Another is not contented with much. Why? God is not there. A little that a righteous man has, says Solomon, is better than great revenues of the wicked.

1. God is the comfort in every creature. It is the word, command, or institution of God, that makes bread to be means of life to us (Matt. 4).

2. He is the source of all comfort that is derived from any aspect of his creation. Listen to Hosea 2:21-23: "And it shall come to pass in that day, I will hear, saith the Lord, I will hear the heavens, and they shall hear the earth. And the earth shall hear the corn, and the wine, and the oil; and they shall hear Jezreel. And I will sow her unto me in the earth; and I will have mercy upon her that had not obtained mercy;

and I will say to them which were not my people, Thou art my people; and they shall say, Thou art my God." Can the bee find anything in the flower without the sun and the rain? It is vain to expect we can obtain any creature comforts without God's influence or impressions first falling on them.

We even lament the loss of such and such a creature because in losing them we believe we have lost the comfort they provided us. But I should rather think that God, having taken them away, is now upon another design, namely, to give more comfort some other way, whether by providential times of afflictions, or through his word and ordained sacraments, or immediately by himself in communication of his spirit. Just as when an earthquake stops the springs on this side the mountain, you may expect them to break out in some other place.

Objection: But if creatures of themselves cannot comfort without God's influence, how do carnal men that have no interest in God rejoice in them?

Answer 1. Some flatter themselves that they have God's blessing because of their enjoyment of worldly comforts. They believe, therefore, that God loves them.

Answer 2. Others fear that they do not have God, and so in the midst of laughter their heart is sad.

Answer 3. Others have neither of those beliefs but are rather atheistic, and so their joy comes in flashes.

And yet still, the truth stands firm. Without God there is no comfort in creatures. And therefore, our surest way is to go to God first if we are to enjoy the comfort that aspects of his creation can bring. Learn to fetch every mercy directly warmed from the hand of God.

Answer 4. Though the saints may need comfort from creatures too, God has reserved himself to be the fountain and dispenser of all comfort to them through everything, in order that our dependence will be in him alone. Blessed be God, the God of all comfort, that has comforted us in all our tribulations, that he may comfort us, and does comfort us, that we may know him as the Author of all comfort. And in doing so we both depend on him and bless him in it. God alone has the key to unlock all comforts, so we must be beholding to him for all. Elijah prayed to God to unlock the clouds that it would rain. The church in Acts 12 prayed to God to unlock the prison doors to let Peter out. The spouse prays in the Song of Songs 1:4 for God to unlock her heart, that it might be unchained and forced to run after him. Therefore, it is a primary spiritual duty in all our enjoyments to consider the motions of our hearts toward God through all comforts than focus on the comforts themselves. It is good to see the beams of divine favor shine glory upon all the clouds of our comforts, but better to allow the streams of them to carry us to the ocean of all, God himself.

Therefore, let us aim at that best thing, that which God most looks at. We see all the creation of plants manifest their dependence on the sunbeams and the drops of rain by shooting up towards heaven. Grace provides the instinct to ascend to that from where it came. We embrace the hand of God when we realize that all creature comforts come first from him. But we ascend up to kiss his face when we see

God as above all, the God of all comfort. Far greater is our sweet communion with the giver than our possession of the gift. We forget the letters and tokens while we embrace our divine husband himself.

See that you answer, then, to God's design. He has set all in a dependence on him, as the lines and circle to a center. Therefore, for all we would have, and for all that we already now have that provide comfort to us, go to God for them, and render back all to God again in praise for them all. Bless him for all. Let your prayers and praises focus on God. Take in all your mercies as accommodations to further you in your journey homeward toward God. Let us delight more in parting with mercies to serve God, our friend, than in keeping them to serve ourselves. As we do so for men, much more then let us do so for God.

In everything give thanks (Phil. 4:6). Let God's blessings be recognized in all, remembering that all God does is to remind you of your dependence on him. When Adam lacked nothing, God gave him a command and a threat to remind him of his dependence. When he left his dependence on God in paradise, he lost everything, as did the very angels in the heaven of glory. As soon as they lost their dependence on God, they fell. How much more should we be reminded of our dependence every minute of the day. And let us conclude that when God sees us growing too fond of our creature comforts and withdraws them from us, it is to turn our attention and dependence once again upon him.

3. Comfort is given to us believers that we might with that, comfort others. We must be like God who

communicates that comfort that is in him. In this way, at once we can have his comfort, and know where it came from in order that we might draw others to go immediately to God for it. This does nothing to diminish our own comfort. But as a candle lighting many shines rather more than less itself, if our own comfort is true, it will communicate itself naturally to others. We are a mystical body, one together in Christ, and therefore our spiritual blood and spirits and warmth must be shared in common.

We often speak of the sweet communion of saints. We feed our own souls when we share our spiritual comforts with others. The very telling of the story of how we were comforted sweetens our comfort on ourselves afresh. In the application and sharing of it with others, we warm our own hearts and spirits. We rub the spices and make them smell more fragrant. Yes, God is as well seen in his streams of comfort running through the ground of our hearts to another's heart, as he was in running into our hearts at first. Therefore, having the first fruits, let us communicate them. The wicked compass sea and land to make proselytes for the devil; we should be doing much more for God, especially considering that he gave you comfort to that end. Everything is elevated in its operations when applied to its utmost end. Our comfort is most glorious, and God is most glorified, the more it comforts others as well as ourselves. It is the same as with a river that it arises at such a fountain and runs so many hundred miles to fortify the valleys and replenish the country as it goes, and then at length falls into the ocean. So is the honor of spiritual comforts in men's hearts.

4. The most excellent comfort and way of comforting is to comfort from experience. God comforts with the comfort he has himself and of himself and so should we comfort others from that which we have from him. The apostle commends experience in Romans 5, when he says that experiential comfort is like a medicine that has been proven effective. Experiential comfort is like the nurse warming the milk in her own mouth before she puts it into the child's.

It warms a disconsolate soul even more so when he hears of another's experiential comforts. For he can say "it is the same God, the same word, the same spirit, the same considerations that comforted him that now speaks to me, and he was the same in every respect as I am. So why should it not comfort me also? Why should I not trust God as well as another? Where or when has God excluded me from comfort more than him?"

Therefore, comforted Christians, draw forth your experiential comforts and serve them to others. As David speaks, "come and I will tell you what the Lord has done for my soul." Waters running through minerals as brimstone, alum, *etc.*, have more strength in them for a physical use. Likewise, comfort is more fitted for men of like frailty as ourselves, and they can take more with them when this comfort has first run through our own hearts, soaked in our own experience, and so communicated with a strong stream of compassions, supplications, and sympathetic consent of spirits. Therefore, examples and experiences often work more readily for us than rules, but the main cause for its effectiveness is that it originated with the God of all comfort. In this way, divine blessing graces it. God appoints the elder Christian as an executor of Christ's testament of comfort to the younger, to exercise his graces and to keep us all united one with another.

5. It is therefore our duty to see that we are God's people, that we may freely take this comfort to ourselves. The apostle describes these to whom he writes in 1 Corinthians 1:1-2 – those who are *called to be saints and sanctified* in Christ Jesus. This necessitates three things. 1) The qualification of God's people, namely, they are saints, they are holy. Holy in conversation (Titus 2:12). They are holy in heart, *i.e.,* the characteristics and temperament of their hearts, as their hearts are purified by faith (Acts 15:9). 2) The same are called to be *saints*. As the apostle says, "you are not called to uncleanness, but to holiness." They have heard a voice in their heart calling them away from their former corrupt condition and conversation into that which is holy; from the world, to look towards heaven; from sin, to Christ. So that they leave all to follow Christ, as the apostles did, at Christ's call. 3) The means by which they are made saints is that they are sanctified in Christ Jesus, not in word only, but by his word and Spirit. They are united to Christ. They reckon themselves (Rom. 6:11) dead to sin in Christ, and alive to God in Christ. All their consideration is to be found in him not having their own righteousness, but the righteousness which is through faith in Christ. He was

made sin for us, and upon him the iniquities of us all were laid, that we might be made the righteousness of God. God's people are those that live recognizing God as the general of their lives (1 Cor. 6:19-20; 2 Cor. 5:15). Those that can with a good conscience plead their sincerity in these things, though not perfection, take the sweet comforts of this doctrine to yourselves. God is the fountain and the Father of mercies, Christ the channel. "Say not who shall ascend up to heaven, to bring God or Christ down thence," (Rom. 10:6-9). You are not under the law, but under grace, (Rom. 6). The God of all comfort has been made your God. This God is the Father of Christ, who is your Savior, Redeemer, and Husband. He is the Father of mercies. Therefore, he takes pity on us and comforts us in all tribulation. He comforts you with enough to overflow to others, so you may comfort them. Pour this oil of gladness over your soul!

He is God; therefore, he is good. Further, he is fully good, as he is infinite in his goodness. He is freely good because he is the first good and is, therefore, exceedingly communicative of that goodness in both creation and regeneration.

He is the Father of our Lord Jesus Christ. As God is the Father of mankind in the first Adam in a natural sense (Luke 3), so he is the Father of believers in and through Christ, the second Adam, in a spiritual sense. As sure as God is united to Christ, so he is to believers (John 14:20, 17:22). As sure as God loves Christ, so he loves those who are in Christ (Matt. 3, Eph. 1:6). As sure as God loves Christ as his son, so Christ loves believers who are also God's children and Christ's brothers and sisters (Heb. 2, John 15:9).

He is the Father of mercies. He will not allow his own to be miserable, except with the intent to be more glorious in his mercy. As the apostle concluded, so many are in unbelief that God might have mercy on them all. And then he adds, "O the depth of the riches, both of the wisdom and knowledge of God!" (Rom. 11:32-33).

With God is no shadow of change, no eclipsing of his beams, and he so infuses believers as stars of the heavens, that they may shine upon things below. He will give comfort to them, and for a witness of it they shall be able to comfort others. They shall see their own comfort was good, and being so comforted, they shall sing forth praise to God for it. Blessed be God that comforts us!

Therefore, you that have not laid claim to this comfort, take it to yourself, grasp it. Do not let discouragement shake you of your comfort. Do as David in Psalm 42 and 43 by asking your soul, "Why are you cast down, o my soul? And why are you disquieted within me? Hope in God, for I shall yet praise him, who is the health of my countenance, and my God." If we have God, the God of all comfort to be ours, why should we be cast down? What can harm us where God will not, or cannot, comfort us? He is the God of all comfort, that comforts in all tribulation. The consideration of this doctrine, and our interest in it, is enough to resolve all doubts as to whether we may cry to him in prayer in times of misery, for he is the Father of mercies.

May we approach him after failings and backslidings? Yes, for he is the Father of mercies.

Can we break under circumstances for lack of his comfort? No! For he is the God of all comfort, that comforts us in all tribulation.

If we fear this affliction, or that trouble, as one cries, "I do not know how I should endure poverty," and another moans, "how shall I deal with my fear of death?" In this is the answer to all cases, God is the God of all comfort and the Father of mercies.

But isn't God just too? Yes, of course. But this is also comforting to a believer that lays hold of his free mercy. 1 John 1:9 says, "If we confess our sins, he is faithful, and just to forgive us our sins, and to cleanse us from all unrighteousness." And 2 Thessalonians 1:6, "it is a righteous, or just thing with God to recompence tribulation to them that trouble you, and to you who are troubled, rest with us..." So, in truth, God's justice is a friend to believers against sins and afflictions.

But God is a God of purity who cannot endure iniquity. And he is a God of power and can choose to crush us in our afflictions. God's goodness is the complexion of his nature and the perfection of all his attributes. Therefore, he is prone to comfort because of his purity as he is pure in his comfort, and by reason of his power as he is powerful in his comforts. Further, he hints to us that it is more suitable to his nature, and more answerable to his direct design, to save and comfort than to condemn and destroy his creature. As John 3:16-17 states, "God so loved the world, that he gave his only begotten son, that whoever believes in him should not perish, but have everlasting life. For God sent not his son into the world, to condemn the world, but that the world through him might be saved." And James 2:13, "Mercy rejoices against judgement." Say then, with the psalmist in Psalm 77:16, "My flesh fails, and my heart fails, but God is the strength of my heart, and my portion forever." For surely God's design is to make his child like himself (in as much as he is willing to communicate himself), to make him full of comfort. He calls us to rejoice (John 15:11; Phil. 4:4; 1 Thess. 5:16). For this reason, when we cry out in need of comfort, we have just cause to cry out against ourselves for not receiving that comfort God that holds out to us, for the joy of the Lord shall be our strength. If the Lord keeps us from despair, and puts us in hope of comfort, that is also a comfort.

But we say we have no comfort because we do not feel it within, and we don't see it work outwardly. But we have hope and life and reason even when we sleep. If we miss comfort, it is enough to say that we have experienced comfort before. And Christ says that our joy shall remain (John 15:11). Though our sight and sense of it does not always appear, it is a sign there is hope for more in that we desire it more.

But you may say you have no joy, and therefore you doubt whether you have Christ. However, a wife is a wife by virtue of her covenant in marriage, even when she is melancholy. And joy may glorify and beautify our spirits more; but to believe in God through Christ, when we have no actual joy, glorifies and honors God more. Pure faith is to trust God without the sense and feeling of it.

But what if you go mourning day after day for comfort and yet cannot attain it? Such desires of comfort argue for grace. Matthew 5 confirms, "Blessed are they that mourn, blessed are they that hunger and thirst for righteousness." It is more of a comfort to be hungry for mercy and think we do not have it than to know we have it, and to be glutted with it, or careless of it.

But you may say you have waited long for comfort, and yet do not have it. Then I tell you to keep the faith, for your comfort will be double in measure and sweetness when it does come, for a desire fulfilled after a long deferring, as Solomon says, is a tree of life.

Do you then wonder what you should do in the meantime? Know that God supports you all the while, and that is great comfort. You have communion with God while waiting; and that also is a great comfort. And finally, believe that you will have plenty of the oil of gladness to ease the wheels of your soul to sustain you for any journey until you are in glory. Amen.

FINIS

Other Helpful Works Published by Puritan Publications

The Nature, Necessity and Character of True Repentance
by Zachary Crofton (1626-1672)

The Christian's Troubles and Deliverance by God
by Thomas Mockett (or Mocket) (1602-1670)

The Good Which Comes Out of the Evil of Affliction
by Nathaniel Vincent (1639-1697)

*The Certainty of Heavenly
and the Uncertainty of Earthly Treasures*
by William Strong (d. 1654)

Four Discoveries of Praise to God
by Alexander Hume (1560-1609)

Armilla Catechetica, or a Chain of Theological Principles
by John Arrowsmith (1602-1659)

A Christian's True Spiritual Worship to Jesus Christ
by Stephen Charnock (1628-1680)

*A Golden Topaz, or Heart-Jewel, Namely, a Conscience
Purified and Pacified by the Blood and Spirit of Christ*
by Francis Whiddon (d. 1656)

www.ingramcontent.com/pod-product-compliance
Lightning Source LLC
LaVergne TN
LVHW041549070426
835507LV00011B/1011